The Charter
of the
Massachusetts
Bay Colony

A Primary Source Investigation
into the 1629 Charter

The Charter of the Massachusetts Bay Colony

A Primary Source Investigation
into the 1629 Charter

Barbara Moe

ROSEN
PRIMARY SOURCE

Published in 2003 by The Rosen Publishing Group, Inc.
29 East 21st Street, New York, NY 10010

First Edition

Library of Congress Cataloging-in-Publication Data
Moe, Barbara A.
The charter of the Massachusetts Bay Colony: a primary
source investigation into the 1629 charter/Barbara Moe.
    p. cm.—(Great American Political Documents)
Includes bibliographical references and index.
Summary: This book describes the events in English history
that led to the Puritans seeking a new country and separating
themselves from the Anglican Church and the problems that
the Massachusetts Bay Colony faced as it became a self-
governing entity.
ISBN 0-8239-3801-8 (lib.)
1. Massachusetts—History—Colonial period, ca. 1600–1775
—Juvenile literature 2. Massachusetts. Charter (1629)—
Juvenile literature 3. Puritans—Massachusetts—History—
17th century—Juvenile literature 4. Massachusetts—Politics
and government—1620–1691—Juvenile literature
 5. Constitutional history—Massachusetts—Juvenile
literature [1. Massachusetts—History—Colonial period, ca.
1600–1775 2. Constitutional history—Massachusetts
3. Puritans]
I. Title II. Series
F67.M75 2003
974.4'02—dc21

                                        2002-151633

Manufactured in the United States of America

Contents

This detail from a painting depicting King Henry VIII's dissolution of the monasteries shows clerics trying to protect what religious reformers thought of as the sinfully accumulated wealth of the established church.

Chapter One

Before They Sailed

And our Will and Pleasure is, and Wee doe hereby for Us, our Heires and Successors, ordeyne and graunte, That from henceforth for ever, there shalbe one Governor, one Deputy Governor, and eighteene Assistants of the same Company, to be from tyme to tyme constituted, elected and chosen out of the Freemen of the saide Company, for the twyme being, in such Manner and Forme as hereafter in theis Presents is expressed, which said Officers shall applie themselves to take Care for the best disposeing and ordering of the generall buysines and Affaires of, for, and concerning the said Landes and Premisses hereby mentioned, to be graunted, and the Plantation thereof, and the Government of the People there.

—The Massachusetts Bay
Colony Charter

The history of the Massachusetts Bay Colony and its charter really began in the sixteenth century with the Protestant Reformation in Europe. As early as the fourteenth century, complaints against the Catholic Church and calls for its reform were widespread. During this period, the Catholic Church had become very powerful, and in fact it was one of the biggest landholders during the Middle

Ages. As a result, many bishops and abbots regarded themselves as secular rulers and were principally concerned with increasing their personal wealth. Corruption in the Catholic Church was widespread, and the clergy had lost a lot of respect. One of the most protested practices was the selling of indulgences by the clergy to raise money. Indulgences were guarantees that sins would be forgiven and that an individual would spend less time in purgatory before taking a certain place in heaven. Indulgences would often be given in large numbers if, for example, there was a need to raise money for a new cathedral, and those who gave, regardless of the state of their souls, were promised salvation.

Protesting a mass granting of indulgences to raise money for the construction of St. Peter's in Rome, on October 31, 1517, a priest named Martin Luther (1483–1546) nailed to the door of All Saints' Church in Wittenberg, Germany, his famous Ninety-Five Theses. This was a long list of the abuses of the Catholic Church.

Originally Luther wanted to reform the Catholic Church from within. But Luther had come to believe that abuses like indulgences were signs of a deeper problem within the church—for instance, its belief that only the clergy could mediate between the people and their god. Luther believed that a church was a group of believers united by faith. The church was its congregation, not the clerical bureaucracy, and any member of the church ought to be able to communicate with his or her God directly. This and other new ideas led to the great split in doctrine, known as the Reformation, between the Catholics and the Protestants.

A woodblock print by the artist Lucas Cranach the Elder depicts Martin Luther, the man who sparked the Protestant Reformation.

Early English Reformers

The Lutheran segment of Protestantism took its name from Martin Luther. But there were many other individuals preaching various programs of religious reform, some of whom came before Luther. One of the issues that disturbed these reformers was

Life of Martin Luther and the Heroes of the Ref

that the Catholic Church permitted the Bible to be printed only in Latin, so that only the educated clergy could read it and interpret the scriptures for the masses. Reformers in England wanted the Bible translated into English so that any literate person

This painting features a composite of scenes from the life of Martin Luther and other prominent figures in the history of the Reformation, including John Wycliffe, the Oxford professor of theology who questioned the absolute authority of the pope almost 200 years before Luther.

could read it. Two of these men were John Wycliffe (1328–1384) and William Tyndale (1494–1536).

John Wycliffe was a professor of theology at Oxford University who questioned the authority of the pope and was expelled from the church for his radical ideas, which preceded Luther's by almost 200 years. Sometime around 1382 he completed a translation of the Bible into English. His followers were known as Lollards, and they traveled around England spreading Wycliffe's ideas. They believed that an organized church was not necessary for salvation and that people could establish a direct relationship with God through prayer. Persecution by the Catholic Church ended the movement. More than forty years

The martyrdom of William Tyndale, who was strangled before being burned at the stake in 1535. Tyndale's crime was printing the New Testament in English.

after Wycliffe's death, the pope ordered that his bones be dug up and burned.

Wycliffe, of course, did his work before the invention of the printing press, and so his Bible was not widely read. In 1524, however, William Tyndale, an English theologian who was an admirer of Luther's, and the liberal scholar Erasmus translated and printed an English version of the New Testament in Worms, Germany. By 1526, copies had been smuggled back into England. Tyndale was arrested in Belgium in 1535 on a charge of heresy. He was condemned to be burned at the stake, but he was strangled before the fire was lit. By then the ranks of the reformers had grown, and they had the support of an English king.

King Henry VIII

King Henry VIII of England came to the throne in 1509. The first of Henry's six wives, Catherine of Aragon, had failed to produce a male heir to the throne. Henry decided to divorce her. When the pope refused Henry's request for a divorce from Catherine, Henry divorced the Roman Catholic Church. In 1543, the Act of Supremacy replaced the pope and made the king head of the Church of England. Some call this act the beginning of the Reformation in England. According to

The title page of Thomas Cranmer's Bible. Cranmer was the Archbishop of Canterbury and a leading figure in the English Protestant movement.

John Fiske in his book *The Beginnings of New England, or, the Puritan Theocracy in its Relation to Civil and Religious Liberty*, Henry succeeded in making England a Protestant nation because the people were already "more than half Protestant in temper." Henry had acted simply out of the need to secure his throne, but the changes he made were historic.

The reign of Henry's son, Edward VI, lasted only seven years. Edward was nine years old when he came to the throne and sixteen when he died. During this time, however, Protestantism became the "official" religion of England, and Thomas Cranmer, archbishop of Canterbury, compiled *The Book of Common Prayer*, which gave the new English church a uniform service that conformed to the new religious ideas.

Queen Mary, who ruled for five years after Edward, married her cousin, the future Philip II, heir to the Spanish throne. Together, Mary and Philip tried to force the Catholic religion back upon England. The persecution of Protestants made Protestantism stronger than ever in England. But the persecution also forced many to flee from England in the mid-1500s. Some ended up in Geneva, Switzerland, where John Calvin (1509–1564) was at the height of his power and influence.

John Calvin

John Calvin proved to be as important to the Reformation as Martin Luther, and he was a major influence on the men and women who first settled at Massachusetts Bay. At the age of twenty-five, Calvin had left France, a Catholic country, and gone to the Protestant city of Geneva, Switzerland. In his

An engraving of John Calvin, a French religious reformer who believed that the fate of Christians was predetermined by God and could not be improved by good works two-volume book, *Institutes of the Christian Religion*, published in 1536, Calvin put forth the doctrine of predestination. The Catholic Church believed that human beings had free will and could choose to be good or evil. Their good acts, including their financial contributions to the church, determined if they would be saved and enter heaven instead of hell. Calvin maintained that God knows in advance everything that will happen in the future and that therefore a person's salvation was determined even before he or she was born. Neither good acts nor priestly rituals would lead to salvation. This did not mean that a person should not perform good acts, but that God, not the church, would determine who was to be saved.

Queen Elizabeth

When Elizabeth became queen of England in 1558 and returned England to Protestantism, many Calvinists and religious reformers were able to return to the country. The queen, though nervous about many of these radical and independent religious groups, such as the Puritans, found herself depending on them. In England's sixteen-year war with Catholic Spain, Elizabeth had to make alliances with other anti-Spanish forces, including the fiercely Protestant Dutch and the Huguenots (French Calvinists). Many English soldiers fighting Spanish armies in Europe came back as Calvinists. Joining the ex-soldiers were Calvinist refugees who set up their churches and held prayer meetings in towns across England. Elizabeth also found herself choosing a number of Puritans for government positions. Finally, a victory over Spain opened the way for English colonization of North America.

Pilgrims, Puritans, and Separatists

Although Puritanism was a movement of religious reform, it was also a way of life. Puritans believed that the Bible was the word of God and tried to live moral lives as they understood the scriptures. Their moral path dictated not only simplicity of worship but also righteousness in daily living. Furthermore, the Puritans assumed that they should be responsible not only for their own strict conduct but also for the conduct of others. They tried to make others believe as they did and had little tolerance for those who did not. This rigid moral behavior was not always appreciated by their neighbors. The character of Malvolio in Shakespeare's

play *Twelfth Night* is a satiric portrait of a Puritan. Malvolio is portrayed as joyless, self-righteous, pompous, and intolerant, and his name means "ill will." Nevertheless, it was the religious convictions of the Puritans that drove the immigration to Massachusetts and led to the type of society that was built there.

The Puritans wanted to eliminate the ceremonies and rituals of the church that were not

The Puritans pray as they prepare to leave exile in Holland to create their own settlements in the New World.

called for in the Bible. They wanted to "purify" the Anglican Church.

But as time went on and they found it impossible to achieve this goal, the Puritans began to think in terms of separating themselves from the church altogether. Some factions of the Puritans came to be known as Separatists, and they were ridiculed and persecuted for their heresies. In 1608, a Separatist group led by William Brewster felt it necessary to leave England and to settle in Leiden, Holland. While missing their former way of life in England, they wanted freedom to worship as they wished. After eleven years, William Brewster led the group back to England, but they sailed for America soon afterward. These Pilgrims founded the Plymouth Colony in North America in 1620.

Eventually the word "Puritan" included such groups as the Presbyterians of Scotland as well as other English religious groups. Some groups, such as those led by John Winthrop, initially conformed to the English style of worship and used *The Book of Common Prayer*. There were also groups known as Nonconformists who disobeyed the law and refused to use the new service in order to worship as they pleased.

After the death of Queen Elizabeth and during the reign of King James I, many Puritans became Separatists and broke with the Church of England. Some were among the group of Pilgrims who sailed on the *Mayflower*. But in spite of their differences, most Puritan groups believed in a simple form of church service and organization.

The Colonial Impulse

In the middle of the sixteenth century, England experienced a steadily increasing commercial expansion. The nation began to compete with Portugal and Spain in exploring the New World. Merchants and traders began to organize into "companies," incorporated bodies that received their authority from the Crown. Acts of Parliament often confirmed these charters, which began the English colonization of America.

These companies were organized in various ways, but the most common and most powerful was the joint-stock company. The constitutions of these companies were similar to those of business corporations today. The members purchased stock in these companies, investing their money and expecting dividends. A governing body ran the company, and shareholders could attend general meetings usually held four times a year. The stock-holders chose the governor and his assistants, who were charged with managing the company.

The stockholders, sometimes called "freemen," and the company officers met in London or other cities to decide how to manage their settlements in America. The colonists themselves might be stockholders or employees of the company. This was clearly a commercial enterprise, but when this system was later transferred to America, as we shall see, it became the foundation for a system of civil government.

A 1609 London Company advertisement sought men and women willing to immigrate to the Jamestown Colony.

Joint-stock companies made possible a concentration of funds, which were necessary to purchase ships and equipment, to employ sailors and captains, and to provide for the settlers until they were able to support themselves in the New World. As a joint-stock company, the Massachusetts Bay Company functioned as a trading corporation that had the powers of ownership and government over a certain geographical area in the Americas. The royal or parliamentary charter granted the company a monopoly over trading rights in that area.

As a result of this commercial expansion, a great migration to North America began in the early 1600s. During this time, tens of thousands of English men, women, and children sailed across the Atlantic Ocean or to the islands of the Caribbean.

There were many reasons that English citizens of the seventeenth century left their homes to settle in unknown regions. Most historians agree that religious motives were primary. Separatists and Dissenters wanted to escape the influence of the official church. At the time, there was little separation of church and state, and religious dissent could lead to prison or worse, depending on how tolerant or strict the policies of the reigning king or queen were.

The political instability of the time added to the desire to seek a new life elsewhere. Almost everyone in England during the late 1620s felt threatened in some way by the policies of Charles I. Military adventures abroad had failed. At home, corruption in government was the rule. When Charles dissolved Parliament in 1629, many felt that there was no longer any hope of making reforms, including the reform of the Anglican Church.

The economic situation also played a part in the decision of many to leave. Low wages, high rents, and government regulation of industry caused economic distress, especially in East Anglia, where the Puritan movement was strong. The enclosure movement drove many farmers from the land and cost them their livelihood. Farmers reasoned that if they could not feel secure in their own country, they might as well try another one. The population of England was also increasing and there was a corresponding rise in unemployment. The idea of economic betterment influenced even the more wealthy Puritans such as John Winthrop. The promise of a new land brought with it hopes for increased earnings from fishing and fur trading, as well as the growing of tobacco and sugarcane.

Chapter Two

The First Settlements

And further, Wee will, and by theis
Presents, for Us, our Heires and Successors,
doe ordeyne and graunte, That the
Governor of the saide Company for the
tyme being, or in his Absence by Occasion
of Sicknes or otherwise, the Deputie
Governor for the tyme being, shall have
Authoritie from tyme to tyme upon all
Occasions, to give order for the assembling of the saide Company, and calling
them together to consult and advise of
the Bussinesses and Affaires of the saide
Company, and that the said Governor,
Deputie Governor, and Assistants of the
saide Company, for the tyme being,
shall or maie once every Moneth, or
oftener at their Pleasures, assemble and
houlde and keepe a Courte or Assemblie
of themselves, for the better ordering
and directing of their Affaires . . .

—The Massachusetts Bay
Colony Charter

Authorities give Captain John Smith credit
for giving the name "New England" to the
six states of the northeast region of North
America. Smith sailed with the group of three ships
that founded the first permanent English settlement
in America at Jamestown, Virginia, in 1607. A
group of London merchants, appropriately called

A portrait of Captain John Smith, an English explorer of North America and one of the founders of the Jamestown Colony in Virginia

the London Company, sponsored the group. Although Jamestown suffered many hardships and disasters, Captain Smith held things together in the difficult years of 1608 and 1609. He also wrote *A Description of New England*, which helped the Pilgrims make their way to Massachusetts.

The most famous legend about Smith involves Pocahontas, daughter of the Indian chief Powhatan. It is said that Pocahontas, not yet a teenager, saved Smith from death at the hands of her father, her uncle, and other tribe members. Although Smith was important in the founding of Virginia and New England, he was unsuccessful in founding a permanent colony at Massachusetts Bay.

In 1619, the first representative legislative body in America met in Jamestown. The London Company authorized the establishment of this House of Burgesses, which consisted of the governor, six counselors, and twenty-two elected members. After six days, the session was adjourned because of hot weather, but not before the legislature had passed laws concerning the religious conversion of Native Americans, a program of agricultural diversification, and the requirement of church attendance. The House of Burgesses modeled itself along the lines of the English Parliament and applied English law to the colony. After King James I died in 1625, no one in England paid much attention to Jamestown and the House of Burgesses. Jamestown

Their ship lying just off shore, the colonists who arrived at Jamestown in 1607 begin to clear the forest and build shelters.

began managing its own affairs and set a precedent for a certain degree of self-government.

The Mayflower Compact

The *Mayflower* sailed from Plymouth, England, in September 1620 and reached the site of Plymouth, Massachusetts, after sixty-five days at sea. The settlers on board, Pilgrims, had planned to land north of Jamestown, but because of bad weather they could not reach that location. The name "Massachusetts" comes from the name of the Indian tribe that lived in the area at the time the Pilgrims arrived. Although the word had many spellings, John Smith reportedly was responsible for the final accepted version. The name means "at the great hill" or "near the great hill," probably a reference to the Great Blue Hill near present-day Boston.

Only a third of those who sailed on the *Mayflower* had been part of the original group of Separatists who had lived in Holland for eleven years. The rest of the group was a mixture. Some people were well educated and had "means," that is, wealth. Others did not. Even before the ship landed, the leaders of the group had decided that rules would be necessary. Forty-one men, seventeen of whom were Separatists who had lived in Leiden,

A painting by the artist Jean Leon Gerome Ferris depicting the signing of the Mayflower Compact in 1620

signed the Mayflower Compact. This document of just under 200 words was not a state constitution and did not set up a government. But it did say that those who signed it would set up a government with rules all would obey. It would help to keep order during difficult times.

Calling King James I "our dread sovereign," the compact declared the signers' intent to make laws and elect officers, and the signers promised obedience to these officers. The compact did not change the social order or the inequalities of wealth between members of the group. It did not give the right to vote to everyone, certainly not to women or to those

A portion of the Mayflower Compact

who did not own property. In reality, the compact was not even legal in the eyes of the British government because the Pilgrims had landed in a different place from the one on which they had received permission to land.

Nevertheless, the Mayflower Compact is an important document in American history. It served as a legal framework for the first ten years of the colony's existence. The members of the Plymouth Colony asked the Council for New England in Britain for a patent that would confirm for the settlers their right to live in the area. Boundary questions were resolved and land deeds secured. The settlers adopted a formal constitution that allowed the shareholders to elect a governor and seven assistants, who had to be church members.

The settlers elected John Carver as their first governor. By the spring of 1621, he had died along with half of the other settlers. William Bradford, who followed him in office, kept his position from 1621 to 1657. In spite of the colony's loyalty to the British Crown, Bradford never succeeded in getting a royal charter. Some historians blame this failure on Bradford's honesty. He had refused to bribe court officials.

The first Thanksgiving took place in the fall of 1621. The Pilgrims invited their Indian friend Massasoit to a feast. He arrived with ninety braves bearing deer meet and turkey. Massasoit signed a peace treaty with the Pilgrims, which lasted until he died forty years later.

The English Civil War

Before discussing the establishment of the Massachusetts Bay Colony, it would be useful to review what was happening in England during this period. James I, who came to the throne in 1603 upon the death of Elizabeth, did not like Parliament, nor did he like the Puritans. In one of his pronouncements he said that the Puritans would "conform" or he would get them out of the land. But the Puritans at this time represented an ever-increasing portion of the English people who had been moving away from the Roman Catholic Church since Elizabeth's struggles with Spain.

In 1625, Charles I, who also disliked the Puritans, succeeded his father, James I, and reigned for twenty-four years. Charles called three Parliaments in four years and dissolved them all when they would not yield to his demands. Not only was there increasing religious conflict between the king and his people, but the king was engaged in a struggle for power with Parliament. Charles believed that he ruled by divine right and held absolute power. Parliament believed that it had rights and powers independent of the Crown. Parliament at this time was dominated by the middle-class gentry and merchants who wanted royal restrictions on trade and financial activity ended. After Charles dissolved Parliament for the third time in 1629, England became an absolute monarchy, governed only by Charles and his advisers. But this led to a civil war from 1642 to 1648. Charles was deposed and executed by Oliver Cromwell and the Parliamentarians, as the revolutionaries were known. The monarchy was not restored until 1660, when Charles II became king.

In his *Compendious History of New England*, written in 1873, John Palfrey points out that the

King Charles I of England receives benediction before his execution in 1649. Below is his death warrant, signed by sixty-seven judges. Charles had tried to oppose the growing trend toward Protestantism among the English people and also tried to assert his absolute authority over the English Parliament. A revolution led by Oliver Cromwell deposed Charles, leading to his execution.

oppressive policies of James I and Charles I raised the political and religious consciousness of the English people. During this period, many thought that their only chance for political or religious freedom would come with a life in the New World. There was a strong impulse to emigrate and take one's chances in the Americas.

John White

John White of Dorchester, England, was a Puritan minister active in civic affairs. In spite of the fact that he never traveled to America, White deserves a great deal of credit for the early successes of the Massachusetts Bay Colony. Because of his position as a clergyman, Reverend White heard much about the possibilities of colonization and about those who had already settled at Plymouth. White wanted to establish another settlement on Massachusetts Bay. Here the people of his native Dorchester could fish, hunt, farm, trade, and practice their religion in peace and freedom. In 1623, White contacted some members of his congregation and others, who formed a joint-stock company called the Dorchester Company of Adventurers. These Puritans needed a new place to settle. Plymouth wouldn't work for them because the Pilgrims at Plymouth had a Separatist orientation.

After deciding to focus on Cape Ann, the Dorchester Company signed up fourteen sailors willing to try to establish a settlement. This venture failed when the company ran out of money. But White would not give up. He managed to get the Dorchester Company's charter transferred to a new group, the New England Company for a Plantation in Massachusetts Bay, better known as the New England Company. The New England Company was a voluntary, unincorporated joint-stock company. In March 1628, a group of people, including the well-known John Endecott, received a grant from the Council for New England for a huge tract of land extending from three miles north of the Merrimac River to three miles south of the Charles River, and from the Atlantic Ocean to the South Sea. This tract of land overlapped territory delineated in several other grants the Council for New England had issued to other groups. When members of the New England Company realized that there was a conflict, they made a decision. Before the council could take back their land, they applied for a royal charter, which would give them a guaranteed title to the land.

Although many people had already given up and dropped out of the venture, White did not. No one knows exactly why he persisted. No doubt he felt the same frustrations as others with the policies and practices of King Charles I. According to the historian J. T. Adams, no one at the time felt safe from the loss of their fortunes or freedom. White was determined to stick with his idea of creating a profitable fishing venture in America. Vicars and curates from all over England, but especially in the eastern counties of England, recruited in person and in letters for the overseas venture.

A portrait of John Endecott, one of the first Massachusetts Bay colonists and governor of the colony until the arrival of John Winthrop in 1630

John Endecott

John Endecott was a Puritan gentleman but also a military man who expected people to obey his commands. John White had made a strong impression on Endecott, who was also from Dorchester. Endecott was a member of the group who got the Council for New

England to grant the land that became home to the Massachusetts Bay Colony.

On June 20, 1628, Endecott sailed on the *Abigail* with a group of forty settlers to Naumkeag, in Massachusetts. Endecott's mission was to establish a settlement similar to the one the Virginia Company had begun at Jamestown twenty years earlier. The settlers soon changed the name of their settlement to Salem, from the Hebrew word "shalom," meaning "peace." Because the New England Company was unincorporated, it could not officially appoint Endecott as governor, but it did name him "chief of command" to succeed the group's first leader, Roger Conant.

Endecott was a strong but impatient man. Stories have him confronting another man of strong temperament, Thomas Morton. Morton, a lawyer and fur trader critical of Puritanism, had set up a trading post at Merrymount where he sold guns and rum to rowdy colonists, pirates, and Native Americans. In the English tradition, Morton had built an eighty-foot maypole. The celebration that followed on May Day, 1627, featured dancing and drinking, which annoyed the Puritans. Because of Endecott's reputation, it's not surprising that many historians have given him credit for chopping down Thomas Morton's maypole at

This painting depicts John Endecott and his supporters breaking up the un-Puritan revelry led by lawyer and fur trader Thomas Morton in 1627.

Merrymount. The famous Puritan Miles Standish had already invaded the settlement and seized those who were drunk, and had taken Morton to Plymouth, from where he was shipped back to England. Some say that Morton got shipped out because of his rivalry for the Indian trade. Several times imprisoned or sent back to England, Morton returned to Massachusetts to oppose Endecott. In the mid-1630s, Morton wrote a book titled *The New English Canaan,* which made fun of the narrow-minded Puritans.

In spite of his faults, Endecott helped to build a successful settlement at Salem. Although many of the settlers died that first winter, Salem became the base for the Great Migration in the years after 1630.

Chapter Three

The Charter of the Massachusetts Bay Company

And, further our Will and Pleasure is, and Wee doe hereby for Us, our Heires and Successors, ordeyne and declare, and graunte to the saide Governor and Company and their Successors, That all and every the Subjects of Us, our Heires or Successors, which shall goe to and inhabite within the saide Landes and Premisses hereby mentioned to be graunted, and every of their Children which shall happen to be borne there, or on the Seas in goeing thither, or retorning from thence, shall have and enjoy all liberties and Immunities of free and naturall Subjects within any of the Domynions of Us, our Heires or Successors, to all Intents, Constructions, and Purposes whatsoever, as if they and everie of them were borne within the Realme of England.

—The Massachusetts Bay
Colony Charter

The government of the new Massachusetts Bay Colony got its authority from the Crown through the Charter of the Massachusetts Bay Company, which some call the First Charter of Massachusetts. The charter was approved on March 4, 1629, and it transformed the New England Company into the Massachusetts Bay Company.

The actual Charter of the Massachusetts Bay Colony signed in 1629. At lower left, a detail from the charter depicts the English king, and at lower right is the official seal that validated the document.

The charter is not easy to read. The English words of that time appear different from the words of today because there were few established spelling rules in the early seventeenth century. People often made up spellings as it suited them, with little concern for consistency. The language is also full of stock phrases, legal expressions, and a certain high-toned religiosity. It has been claimed that the pious forms and phrases were "reverent" because the petitioners wanted to form not only a profit-making company but also a godly one.

The charter stated that the stockholders, or "freemen," would meet once every quarter, or four times a year, in a general court to make laws for the company and the colony. Once a year at one of these meetings, the freemen would choose a governor, a deputy governor, and eighteen assistants or directors for the coming year. This executive council was supposed to meet every month to manage business matters. The governor or his deputy governor and at least six assistants were to be present at any meeting of the general court in order to make valid decisions. Just seven people would be able to exercise the powers of the general court. The general court could admit new freemen and make new laws. The only stipulation was that these laws must not conflict with English laws. Freemen were expected to attend meetings, serve on committees, vote, and accept offices to which they were appointed or elected. If they refused, they could be fined.

We know that the Massachusetts Bay Company was a trading company organized to establish a colony in America both as a profit-making corporation and as a religious settlement. It was meant to be governed from England, as was any company created for trade and colonization. But a number of the Puritans had other ideas. The members of the group were not all of the same degree of Puritan persuasion. Most of those from London and the western part of England still wanted to conform to the Church of England's practices. Though they were Protestants, they were known as Congregationalists because of their willingness to accept the rituals of the Anglican Church. Those from the East Anglia region tended to be Separatists or Nonconformists. As a group, however, they were united in their goal to establish a successful colony. Among them were Emanuel Downing, Isaac Johnson, Thomas Dudley, and John Winthrop.

John Winthrop

John Winthrop was the best-known of the governors who contributed to the success of the Massachusetts

A portrait of John Winthrop, who governed the Massachusetts Bay Colony, from 1630 periodically until 1649. Both Winthrop's son and grandson eventually served as governors of the colony as well.

Bay Colony. Winthrop also contributed a son and grandson to the building of New England. Both at different times served as governor of the colony. The Massachusetts Bay Colony's long-term governor eventually married four times and had sixteen children. Winthrop left his own records of his life and times. These records include his journal, which was published in 1908 as *The History of New England from 1630 to 1649*. As a leader, Winthrop was smart, personable, energetic, resourceful, and not easily daunted.

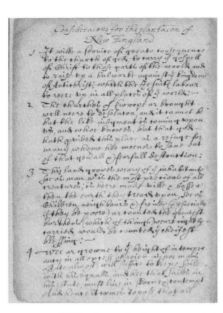

The opening page of John Winthrop's *Considerations for the Plantation of New England*. Winthrop desired to create a religious state based on Puritan principles in the New World.

Winthrop's dream, which he believed was God's will and which he pursued until he died, was to create a Puritan religious state in the New World. Winthrop's dream is often misunderstood today. He and his followers did not intend to create a state in which different religious beliefs or non-beliefs could exist side-by-side. In fact, the opposite was true. For Winthrop, being a loyal citizen meant having specific religious beliefs and forms of worship. Anyone who did not agree with these policies was free to leave.

In England, Winthrop had never been a poor man. He was a country gentleman and a landowner who graduated from Cambridge and became a lawyer like his father. Many of the other leaders with whom Winthrop worked in founding the Massachusetts Bay

Colony were also men of political, intellectual, and social standing. In fact, this would be the biggest and most important group ever to leave England. United in a single-minded religious and political purpose, they felt that God had commissioned them to do this work.

In July 1629, Winthrop had taken a horseback ride north to Lincolnshire, England, with his brother-in-law Emanuel Downing. Here they conferred with the earl of Lincoln and several other prominent Puritans. Isaac Johnson, the earl's brother-in-law, had called the meeting to discuss an extraordinary idea, moving the location of the charter.

Other companies like the Massachusetts Bay Company had powers over various settlements in America. They held meetings in London, Plymouth, or whatever English city their charters specified. They then sent governors across the ocean to enforce the rules. This was the assumption when the Massachusetts Bay Colony got its charter, but it was only an assumption. Because of an apparent oversight, the charter had failed to prescribe a meeting place for the company.

The Cambridge Agreement

As governor of the company, Matthew Craddock wanted to make the settlement-to-be independent of the company. He and others feared interference from Sir Fernando Gorges, who had competing plans and was not sympathetic to the Puritans' project. Some had argued that to make the settlement independent of the company would be contrary to the intent of the charter and therefore illegal. On the other hand, many argued that not only should governing powers be transferred but that the whole company should move. As a result of these discussions, twelve men, including John Winthrop and Thomas Dudley, met at Cambridge on August 26, 1629. They agreed to leave for the New World by March 1, 1630.

The men reasoned that if the company continued to meet in England, the king could find things to quarrel about and could possibly take back the charter. This had happened to the Virginia Company of London. Taking the charter with them to America would remove much of the king's power to interfere in their affairs. The company could erect a self-governing religious commonwealth. It would allow the leaders to create the kind of society they wanted, a "City of God in the wilderness."

The Cambridge Agreement was presented at a meeting of the general court. On August 28, 1629, two groups argued for and against it. At the vote the next day, only 27 members out of a total of 125 were present to vote, and the motion passed.

Winthrop was not a member of the New England Company. But now his name began to appear on documents of the time. As other men retired, he became a leader of the group that planned to create a self-governing, independent Puritan state in America. A new experiment was beginning. At a general court on October 20, 1629, John Winthrop was elected governor of the Massachusetts Bay Company.

In the fall and winter of 1629, the hard work of preparation for the voyage began. Not everyone preparing to leave was a Puritan. Some potential settlers were young men in search of adventure, economic opportunity, or freedom. Many signed on to perform the necessary practical tasks of any such voyage—outfitting the ships and getting supplies such as equipment and food. The colonists took clothing, furniture, household utensils, nails, tools, guns, and other items for trading, as well as beer and wine.

After his election as governor, Winthrop had to take charge of all preparations for the trip, including picking the passengers. He could not pick only those with the proper Puritan credentials. He needed skilled craftsmen. Some planters or adventurers paid their own way and would be able to buy a piece of land in America. Others were recruited as indentured servants. These were usually young men who came to the New World willing to perform service for a period for a master who had paid their passage. Most agreed to work for seven years, but some skilled workers had to remain indentured for only three years.

In the seventeenth and eighteenth centuries, masters were expected to house, feed, and clothe their servants and to treat them with kindness, or at least not with cruelty. The master expected the indentured servant to work hard, not to marry without the master's permission, and not to run away. Indentured servitude was a fact of life in all of the colonies, but it was more common in those that grew crops such as tobacco on large plantations where the owner's family could not provide enough labor itself.

Sailing

On March 29, 1630, eleven ships gathered at the harbors of Southampton and Plymouth. All together there were a thousand passengers—men, women, and children—along with cows, horses, goats, pigs,

This nineteenth-century painting depicts John Winthrop standing on the deck of the *Arbella* off the shore of Salem, Massachusetts, in 1630, preparing to land in the New World.

and chickens. The group that left first consisted of the lead ship, the *Arbella*, and three others. Winthrop, his sons Adam and Stephen, and the charter sailed on the *Arbella*. Winthrop's wife, Margaret, who was expecting another child, had stayed behind temporarily. The couple's son John Jr., twenty-three years old, stayed with her and the other children to settle the family's affairs. Winthrop and Margaret had agreed to think of each other every Monday and Friday at 5 PM.

Earlier in London, John Winthrop had taken over from Matthew Craddock as governor of the company. As he began his journey, Winthrop started his journal. Filled with religious energy, worried about the end of the world as he knew it, plagued with financial problems, and passed over for a job in the English government, Winthrop was ready to start a new life in the New World.

The voyage lasted approximately two months. While en route, Winthrop delivered a stirring sermon called "A Model of Christian Charity," which included this often-quoted line: ". . . to do justly, to love mercy, and to walk humbly with our God." In the sermon, Winthrop clearly stated the vision and principles guiding the leaders of the colony, which would have the eyes of the world upon it. One important principle was the yielding of individual privileges for the good of the community. The rights of the individual would be subordinate to the common good.

The first ships landed at Salem but did not stay long because conditions there did not look favorable. Not only were the new arrivals hungry, malnourished, and in danger of succumbing to scurvy, so were those already settled in Salem. The settlers were equally hungry and living in huts or in wigwams. They were fearful of the Native Americans, who

The actual remains of the *Sparrow-Hawk*, a small vessel that brought twenty-five colonists to the New World in 1626. They were bound for Virginia, but a storm left them stranded at Cape Cod, where they were rescued by William Bradford.

owned guns obtained from traders who had come before. In spite of the beauty of the natural surroundings, many of the new arrivals were ready to pack up and head for home.

During the early days, Winthrop had little time to write letters to Margaret or to make entries in his journal. And yet Winthrop himself had no doubts about his mission and never considered giving up. As he searched for a new place to settle in the area, his confidence inspired the same in others. Winthrop explored Massachusetts Bay, including the peninsula of Charlestown, where he decided to move his people. Ultimately, groups of settlers spread out and founded "plantations," which soon dotted the bay. As Winthrop tried to find corn and other foods to support the group, the settlers found shelter in existing caves dug into hillsides and made cellars that they covered with roofs. A few made wigwams or built frame houses. Winthrop and some of the other leaders lived in a house already constructed.

But there was much sickness in Charlestown. Blaming the water supply, Winthrop and others crossed the peninsula, where they founded the city of Boston. People were still hungry and many became sick and died, but Boston grew and became the economic and political center of the colony.

The Pilgrims arrive at Plymouth Harbor and begin to explore their new environment. In the left of the picture, a Native American looks on anxiously.

In spite of losing eleven servants that he considered part of his family, Winthrop remained healthy and kept his spirits up. But others, trying to survive that first winter, did not keep their spirits up and did not stay. By February, widespread starvation seemed inevitable. But a ship arrived with fresh supplies and enough lemon juice to prevent scurvy. When the ship left, however, it took eighty people back to England. Two hundred more settlers died that winter.

Much to Winthrop's disappointment, word had gotten back to England about the hardships. Many who had planned to come changed their plans. But with the arrival of spring and fresh supplies, the colonists began to plant crops. Because most of the Massachusetts settlements were close to the sea, people were able to count on fish for nourishment and for trade. For the settlers of the Massachusetts Bay Colony, there was never as bad a winter as the first.

In the fall of 1631, Margaret Winthrop arrived with the rest of the couple's children. Perhaps her safe passage signaled the start of better times ahead. Although only a few settlers came in the period between 1631 and 1632, the next year was a banner year for the colony. That year in England, Bishop Laud was made the archbishop of Canterbury. He suppressed all Puritan activities to such an extent that many felt they had no choice but to leave. The Great Migration had begun. By the end of the 1630s, 20,000 people had arrived in New England.

How They Lived

Eventually the settlers moved out of their caves and wigwams and built simple cottages with a single room for living and cooking and a loft for sleeping. Later, those who could afford a second room added one. Sometime later, a different type of house, the "salt box," appeared. This house had a cellar with a

The lives of the first colonists were full of hardship and hazards. The land had to be cleared and homes had to be built. The colonists also had to plant crops and hunt game until the crops thrived. Many of the early colonists died of disease and starvation.

raised ground floor and a kitchen at the back. Rush mats on the floors added to simple wooden tables, benches, and beds.

The Puritans of the Massachusetts Bay Colony had to work hard to survive. But Puritans were not the sour-faced fun-haters they have often been accused of being. They loved reading, especially history and the Bible. They also liked to hunt, fish, and sing. They liked to eat and were not against drinking in moderation. They did not dress only in gray and black.

A reconstruction of the original colony stands at Plymouth today. A great effort has been made to duplicate the details of the living arrangements as closely as possible to what they were in the 1620s.

Large families were the rule and made up for the decrease in immigration after 1640. Because of their special covenant with God to live saintly lives, the Puritans could not leave sins unpunished. This rule carried over into family life. All family members had to attend church whether or not they wanted to.

Chapter Four

Troubles and Successes

And, Wee doe of our further Grace, certen Knowledg and meere Motion, give and graunte to the saide Governor and Company, and their Successors, That it shall and maie be lawfull, to and for the Governor or Deputie Governor, and such of the Assistants and Freemen of the said Company for the Tyme being as shalbe assembled in any of their generall Courts aforesaide, or in any other Courtes to be specially sumoned and assembled for that Purpose, or the greater Parte of them (whereof the Governor or Deputie Governor, and six of the Assistants to be alwaies seaven) from tyme to tyme, to make, ordeine, and establishe all Manner of wholesome and reasonable Orders, Lawes, Statutes, and Ordinances, Directions, and Instructions, not contrairie to the Lawes of this our Realme of England . . .

—The Massachusetts Bay
Colony Charter

In the Massachusetts Bay area of New England, an English trading company from London transformed itself into a commonwealth, independent and self-governing. In this transformation, however, many human failings, prejudices, and passions played a part.

In Charlestown, on August 23, 1630, the first court of assistants, or magistrates as they came to be known, was held. The assistants appointed justices of the peace to punish offenders and to make rules for the court meetings to be held every month.

The people brought their ideas for government with them, but they also developed new ideas as time went on. They wanted free debate, free elections, and the right to petition their legislative assembly. They added their own Puritan notions about the sinfulness of man and the necessity for God's redemption. For a while, their only guide was the charter, which had not been created for the self-governing system that they now needed.

In the first years of the colony, the governor, his deputy, and the assistants had made pronouncements and had overseen matters of government. Winthrop believed that for the colony's own good such centralization of power was needed. John Winthrop, at least during this period of history, was a believer in strong government by the leaders, not necessarily in government by the people. Winthrop believed that a few should rule and the rest should be ruled. Some felt that Winthrop was too authoritarian. Others thought that he was too lenient.

However, the charter did call for the meeting of a general court every quarter with freemen in attendance to make laws and admit other freemen. So far no courts had been held, and the only freemen in the colony were those in the court of assistants. When a call went out for people who needed no special qualifications for membership, 108 men responded. At the May meeting, however, it was decided that from then on no one could be admitted as a freeman who did not belong to the church. Although this requirement violated the charter, Winthrop and others were apparently afraid that opening up membership could change the goals of the colony and alter its religious composition.

In 1632, the people made themselves heard when the church at Watertown protested the imposition of a tax by the court of assistants at Boston for the making of a protective fence around the new town of Cambridge. According to the charter, the governor and assistants did not have the authority to levy taxes. Winthrop got around this protest by saying that the colony was not a corporation but a commonwealth, and that the body that levied the tax was similar to a parliament.

In the same year, the colony created its own public stock as a way of meeting expenses. In addition, sixteen persons, two each from eight settlements, would be appointed to give advice to the governor and assistants about introducing a system of taxation. Although this consultative committee was disbanded as soon as it had done its work, it was the first time that the towns had played a part in addressing such an important issue.

Trouble for Winthrop

So far the freemen had obtained the right to help elect the governor and to participate in matters of taxation in the general court. But the charter had given them the right to meet four times a year to help make laws and ordinances. Some colonists began to realize that Governor Winthrop and his assistants had been making laws, distributing lands, raising money, and punishing offenders without the consent of the settlers and in violation of the charter.

In 1634, Israel Stoughton complained to his brother in England that Winthrop had taken too much upon himself. The subsequent revolt against Winthrop was not a sudden one, however. At a meeting of the general court many issues were reviewed in long and stormy sessions. Finally the freemen could take credit for several gains, including a new freeman's oath and a ruling that only they could raise money, levy taxes, dispose of lands, and confirm titles. But they considered their greatest victory a new privilege, that in each town the freemen could choose two of three of their group to represent them in three out of four of the general courts. For the fourth meeting in May, the election meeting, the freemen had to report in person.

Empowered by their victory, the freemen voted Winthrop out of office—if only temporarily—and for the next three years they elected three different men who were far less flexible than their predecessor. The first was Thomas Dudley, Winthrop's former deputy. The following year, 1635, they elected John Haynes, and in 1636 they elected the twenty-three-year-old Henry Vane.

In 1637, however, they reelected Winthrop, who had only one other two-year-long interruption in his services as governor until he died in 1649. By the time of Winthrop's reelection, the colony had become a self-governing entity built on a constitutional framework, with power vested in a governor, a deputy governor, their assistants, and a general court. Although the commonwealth professed obedience to the king, the leaders feared his interference.

Around 1634, opponents in England had begun to threaten the colonial leaders. Archbishop Laud, a rather disagreeable churchman, especially to those who did not believe as he did, headed a committee to look into the independent activities of the Massachusetts Bay Colony. When the committee figured out that the charter had traveled to America with the settlers, the group ruled in favor of Charles I, who declared that now he would govern the colony. Fortunately for the colony, Charles I could not follow up on his threats because he kept dissolving Parliament and was having more than enough trouble governing his own country. But the threats from England continued.

Religious Troubles

Although the colony's leaders wanted religious freedom on their own terms, they did not want diversity and tried to squash it. Nevertheless, divisions did arise. Roger Williams, a Londoner, had arrived in the Massachusetts Bay Colony at the age of twenty-eight. Although he had been involved in the Massachusetts Bay project for as long as Winthrop, Williams did not come with Winthrop in the spring of 1630. He arrived in February 1631 during the first horrible winter. Educated as a clergyman, Williams did not at first

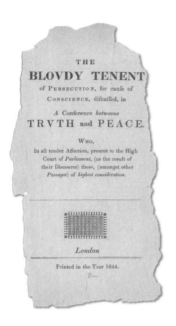

The title page of the pamphlet *The Bloody Tenent of Persecution* by Roger Williams. Williams was a colonist who arrived in Massachusetts in 1631 and attacked the religious intolerance of men like Governor John Winthrop.

accept a minister's position because he considered the church dishonest in many ways. Williams, an avowed Separatist as well as a kind man, felt no allegiance to the Church of England. Furthermore, he did not want to lead in worship people who refused to renounce the Anglican Church. He asserted that the charter of this colony was not legitimate. He wondered how the Crown could grant land that England didn't own. He suggested that the charter be sent back to the king. He also believed that no one should be punished for religious beliefs different from those of the majority. For his beliefs and pronouncements, the leaders of the Massachusetts Bay Colony ultimately banned Williams from the colony. In early 1636, he fled into the wilderness and later bought land from the Native Americans with whom he had always been friendly. Eventually, Williams founded Providence, which became the capital of Rhode Island.

Another threat to the colony was the Antinomian controversy that occurred between 1634 and 1637. Even before the colony had gotten rid of Roger Williams, the Puritans found that another outspoken

person was in their midst. Antinomian Anne Hutchinson had arrived in Boston in 1634 with her husband and children. That she did not hesitate to express her views was one thing, but that she was a woman expressing such views was almost unbearable to the male leaders of the Massachusetts Bay Colony. Hutchinson and those who agreed with her challenged the

The trial of Anne Hutchinson, who was banished from the Massachusetts Bay Colony in 1637. Hutchinson was an antinomian who opposed strict Puritan religious principles.

strict religious views, policies, and forms of worship of Winthrop and his followers. The antinomians argued for a personal and direct relationship with God. Not helping Hutchinson's cause was her claim that she had the gift of prophecy. The Puritans of the Massachusetts Bay Colony banished her from the colony in 1637.

Because the colony's leaders did not welcome challenges to their congregationalist views, they felt threatened by those with different religious views, such as Presbyterians, Anabaptists, and members of the Society of Friends (Quakers).

The Pequot War

The population of the Massachusetts Bay Colony, which had grown into a collection of towns and settlements, rose from about 4,000 people in 1634 to approximately 11,000 by 1638. This population increase and the resulting expansion of settled land put pressure on the neighboring Pequot tribe of Native Americans. Thomas Hooker, a liberal minister who clashed with the Puritans, led the establishment of Hartford in what is now Connecticut. The English Saybrook Company established Fort Saybrook, which was near the Pequot village of Mystic. Roger

Williams, who even in his exile from the Massachusetts Bay Colony had maintained contact with John Winthrop, warned Winthrop of the possibility of conflict with the Indians.

The Pequot War, which began in 1637, was New England's first major war. Historian Alden Vaughan says that "brilliant diplomacy" might have prevented the war, but no one was up to the task. Although the colonists had earlier negotiated a treaty with the Pequots, many wanted to break it. Their opportunity came when someone killed two colonists. The Pequots denied involvement. But the magistrates of Massachusetts Bay ordered Endecott, who took along a hundred volunteers, to Block Island (Rhode Island) to kill all of the Pequot men, guilty or innocent. When Endecott couldn't find the hiding natives, he burned their wigwams and left. Retaliation followed retaliation.

Finally, the General Court of Massachusetts and the Connecticut Court both declared war on the Pequot tribe. Forces of the courts joined with Native American allies to wage war, much of which took place in the Connecticut Valley. By 1636, the Massachusetts Bay Colony had developed a huge military force. A surprise attack by the Puritan forces at a Pequot fort on the Mystic River turned

Massachusetts colonists attack a Pequot fort. The Pequot War, which began in 1637, resulted in the near-extermination of the entire tribe.

into a burning of the village, with English soldiers shooting anyone who tried to escape. The troops wiped out the entire Pequot tribe, including men, women, and children—up to 700 in all. Some survivors were taken as servants or sent to the West Indies. In 1638, the Treaty of Hartford ended the war. This treaty with allied tribes as signers declared the end of the Pequot tribe and opened the way for colonization of the Connecticut coast. For the next thirty-eight years, there were no more wars.

The Founding of Harvard College

Most of the clergy and some of the settlers of the Massachusetts Bay Colony had graduated from Cambridge University in England. By 1636, many wanted to establish a university in the new colony. The general court agreed, appropriated £400 for the purpose, and chose a site for the college at Newton, where the college opened its doors in 1638.

An artist's view of Harvard College in 1668. It lay to the north of the Charles River in Boston.

In May 1637, John Harvard had arrived in Charlestown, Massachusetts, with his wife, Ann. Little is known about John Harvard, but he was born in London and didn't start college himself until he was twenty. A little over a year after arriving in Charlestown, on September 14, 1638, he died of tuberculosis at the age of thirty-one. Harvard had willed his library collection and half of the rest of his estate to the college. In gratitude, the college took Harvard's name, and in honor of Cambridge, England, leaders changed the town's name to Cambridge.

The Growth of Self-Government

The growth of towns and villages had made self-government even more necessary than before. In 1641, the general court approved a legal code for the colony. The document, primarily the work of Nathaniel Ward, a former attorney from Ipswich, was known as the Body of Liberties. As a kind of bill of rights, it served as a guide for the colonists until a more comprehensive document could be prepared. Ward based much of the code on English law, but the code also contained items specific to New England. For example, for all practical purposes the code excluded the practice of law, and it prohibited cruelty to animals. Because many believed the code gave too much power to a few men, it was never published.

A confederation of four colonial regions—Massachusetts, Plymouth, Connecticut, and New Haven—organized in 1643 shows the desire for discussion and cooperation among these groups. Called the United Colonies of New England or the New England Federation, the organizers hoped to form a "league of friendship" to mutually protect them from attacks by the Dutch, French, and Native Americans, and to solve boundary disputes.

In 1648, the court adopted an improved version of the Body of Liberties and called it *The General*

A page from *The General Laws and Liberties of the Massachusets Colony,* adopted in 1648. The laws specified penalties for committing idolatry, blasphemy, and witchcraft, among other crimes. This page is from an edition published in 1672.

Laws and Liberties of the Massachusets Colony. The fifty-nine pages, an alphabetical collection of laws, incorporated parts of the Body of Liberties that had not been repealed, as well as other general laws. Although a listing such as this one had been used in England before, this first volume published in America was so complete that it bound judges to abide by definite standards.

King Philip's War

In the spring of 1675, life in the Massachusetts Bay Colony was going well. But another tragic war with the Indians threatened this peace. Unhappy people on both sides stirred things up. One discontented person was Metacomet, also named Philip, who was sachem, or chief, of the Wampanoag tribe. Metacomet was one of the sons of Massasoit, who had befriended the early settlers. But the colonists had not treated Massasoit's sons as well as their father had treated the colonists. Many of the colonists were hungry for Indian lands. "King Philip," as the colonists called him, began to believe he had to drive out the white men and their families. Before the war ended, an estimated 5,000 Native Americans had died. The

Puritans also suffered casualties and a dozen of their towns were destroyed or deserted.

The Restoration

The restoration of the Stuart dynasty to the English throne in 1660 caused a battle of wills between the Crown and the colony. King Charles II demanded that the colonists trade only with England. When the leaders of the Massachusetts Bay Colony refused, Charles canceled their charter in 1684.

In 1691, King William III made a new charter for the Massachusetts Bay Colony, which gave the people some privileges but ended the colony's independence. Although the colonists kept their land titles, could hold town meetings, and could participate in the making of laws, the king would now appoint the governor and have the veto power over colonial decisions. This so-called provincial period in the history of Massachusetts lasted until 1776 and the American Revolution.

Chapter Five

The Colonists and the Rights of Others

And Wee doe further, for Us, our Heires and
Successors, give and graunt to the said Governor
and Company, and their Successors by theis Presents, that all and everie such Chiefe Comaunders, Captaines, Governors, and other Officers
and Ministers, as by the said Orders, Lawes,
Statuts, Ordinances, Instructions, or Directions
of the said Governor and Company for the Tyme
being, shalbe from Tyme to Tyme hereafter
imploied either in the Government of the saide
Inhabitants and Plantation, or in the Waye by
Sea thither, or from thence, according to the
Natures and Lymitts of their Offices and Places
respectively, shall from Tyme to Tyme hereafter
for ever, within the Precincts and Partes of Newe
England hereby mentioned to be graunted and
confirmed, or in the Waie by Sea thither, or from
thence, have full and Absolute Power and
Authoritie to correct, punishe, pardon, governe,
and rule all such the Subjects of Us, our Heires
and Successors . . .

—The Massachusetts Bay
Colony Charter

The Charter of the Massachusetts Bay
Colony speaks of a commitment to win
over Indians to a belief in the Christian
faith. The laws of Massachusetts, as well as those of
Plymouth and Connecticut, show the desire, in
theory at least, of the colonists to deal fairly with
the Native Americans.

Some of the settlers tried to fulfill their promises to convert the Native Americans to Christianity, to "civilize" them, and to give them an education. Beginning in about 1643 on the islands of Nantucket and Martha's Vineyard, Thomas Mayhew tried to persuade many of the Indians to believe in the one Christian god and to teach the children to read and write. In 1646, Massachusetts enacted a law that each church should pick two church members to spread the gospel. In 1649, Parliament set up the Society for Propagating the Gospel in New England. Harvard College wanted to enroll Native Americans, but in the early days only one, Caleb Cheeshahteaumuck, took advantage of the offer and graduated.

This push to "civilize" the Native Americans occurred frequently in colonial territories around the world that were settled by Europeans. Though the motives of the colonists were complex, and many genuinely believed in helping the Indians, the basic notion was part of a larger idea that justified the presence of European settlers on other people's lands. Before the arrival of the colonists, the Americas were defined as a wilderness, as if a thousand years of Native American civilization never existed. The "civilizing" impulse justified the establishment and

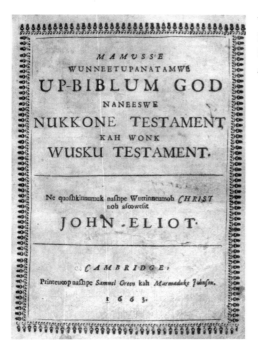

expansion of the European colonies and gave the colonists a justification for taking Indian lands.

John Eliot, who had come to Massachusetts in 1631, learned the Algonquian language and in 1646 began his work as a missionary at an Indian village near Watertown. He established Indian villages that came to be called praying towns, where like-minded Native Americans would live together and come in contact only with "Christian influences." In 1651, a stockaded village was set up at Natick. Directed by an English carpenter, the Indians built colonial-style log houses. Many wore their hair short and adopted

English dress. By 1674, the number of "praying Indians" in the area had reached approximately 4,000.

Up to the time of King Philip's War, it appeared that relations between the Puritans and the Algonquian tribes were at least civil. The native tribes, however, must have felt totally frustrated by the expansionist pressure of the colonists. It did not matter that John Eliot's intentions were honorable and benevolent. When the most powerful tribes of the region saw the smallest and weakest tribe, the Massachusett Indians, being gathered into villages, learning about a strange new god, and wearing unusual clothing, they may have thought that their brothers were being conscripted to help the Puritan military forces. In 1657, when Eliot preached a sermon to the men of one of the small tribes and asked if they would accept Jesus Christ as their savior, the Indians reportedly refused. It was remarkable that peace between the Native Americans and the colonists could have lasted for thirty-eight years, but the memory of what happened to the Pequots in 1637 kept Indian frustrations under wraps.

The interaction between the colonists and the Native Americans, however, clearly threatened Indian culture and traditions. Puritan expansion encroached on the land of native peoples, and many Indian chiefs experienced a weakening of their leadership and power. Some tribes began to depend on trade with the colonists, and King Philip's War wiped off the map most of the Indian tribes of central and southern New England.

Both the English and the Dutch colonists tried to use Native Americans as slaves. Wall Street in New York City was named because of the wall the Dutch settlers used to keep Indian slaves in and their relatives out. In the middle of the 1600s, the colonists of Massachusetts began to think that Native American slaves might solve their labor problems. But the type of farming done in New England did not lend itself to the use of slaves, nor did the Indians prove to be good "slave material." Some refused to "cooperate" and others just died.

Africans

The seventeenth century in America also saw the beginnings of slavery, not only of Native Americans but also of Africans. Indentured servitude had been the main source of labor for most of the colonies in the early seventeenth century. But indentured servitude, from the master's point of view, had many disadvantages. After serving for anywhere from three or four to seven or more years, indentured

A slave trader shows off his cargo to settlers of the Virginia Colony. Virginia planters began to depend upon slavery in the middle of the seventeenth century when the supply of indentured servants started to dwindle.

servants completed their contracts and were free to farm their own land. As there was so much available land in the New World, there was no incentive to stay with a former master and work his land, even for a wage. In a fairly short time, generations of indentured servants finished their labor contracts and moved on, and the wealthier farmers found themselves facing a labor shortage.

The colonists began to look south, toward the colonies originally established by the Spanish in the West Indies, where slaves had been imported from Africa after the native populations of the Caribbean islands had been worked to death. The cost of maintaining slaves was much lower than the cost of indentured servants, but they could double their owners' income. Gradually the colonists began to import slaves, especially in the southern colonies where large plantations produced tobacco for export back to England. But the merchants of New England also profited from the slave trade.

Women

Women did play a part in shaping the Massachusetts Bay Colony. Women often challenged the prevailing policies and narrow belief systems.

After the Massachusetts authorities kicked out Anne Hutchinson, another Anne appeared in the colony. Anne Dudley Bradstreet was the daughter of Winthrop's deputy governor, Thomas Dudley, and the wife of a Massachusetts assistant, Simon Bradstreet. She did not write sermons as Hutchinson did. Instead she wrote poetry. While functioning as a wife and mother, Bradstreet wrote verses that gave voice to her fears and to the fears of other women, such as the fear of death in childbirth. She also wrote about her frustrations, one of which was undoubtedly the oppression she felt as a woman in a "man's world."

In 1638, Boston acquired the first printing press in the Americas, but it was used only for religious materials and official documents. Nevertheless, the Massachusetts Bay Colony was in some ways a literary community. Even though the Puritans banned frivolous works such as novels, plays, and poetry unless the works had a religious message, they were educated people.

In 1656, two other brave women came to the Massachusetts Bay Colony. Ann Austin, the mother of five children, and Mary Fisher, her young maid, intended to preach their Quaker beliefs. Instead, the colonial authorities burned their books and threw the two women into a Salem prison. Soon thereafter,

Mary Prince, as part of a group of eight Quakers, arrived in Boston. They also spent time in prison as they awaited their shipment back to England because they had expressed their beliefs. When Mary Prince complained about her sentence to Governor Endecott, he tried to talk her out of her beliefs. Magistrates at that time practiced equality in one sphere: They threw out Quakers of both sexes. Anyone who persisted in coming back to the colony got another violation. Four violations led to the death sentence.

Quaker women were not known for keeping their thoughts to themselves. Twenty years after Anne Hutchinson left Massachusetts, her sister Katherine Scott arrived. Because Scott spoke out for the equality of all people, Governor Endecott sentenced her to ten lashes at the whipping post. In her three trips to Boston, former antinomian-turned-Quaker Mary Dyer spoke out against Puritan beliefs. She was whipped, imprisoned, banished from the colony, and finally hanged.

According to Lyle Koehler, author of *A Search for Power: The "Weaker Sex" in Seventeenth-Century New England,* there are many surprising stories about women of the Puritan era. Consider, for example, the stories of Deborah Wilson and Lydia Wardell. Walking naked in Salem in 1662, Wilson explained that she was protesting the practice of stripping Quaker women to the waist and whipping them in public. To punish her, the magistrates forced her to walk again through Salem tied to a garbage cart with her upper body exposed. Every so often the constable walking behind her gave her a few lashes with his whip. The following year, when church leaders asked Lydia Wardell why she had not been coming to Sunday services, she showed up at church naked. She explained this behavior by saying that she wanted to wake up the leaders to their own ignorance.

Not all the women of seventeenth century Massachusetts were as assertive. Some women had mental disorders, which may have been caused by anxiety due to repression. These women brought grief to the colony in the form of "witch trials," most notably the ones in Salem in the winter of 1691 to 1692. It was not unusual at the time for people to tell fortunes based, for example, on the shape of a raw egg dropped into a cup of water. Such superstitious practices enabled a few young girls to have hysterical "fits." People began to call others witches when they claimed to be able to make others well or sick, to predict the future, to cast a spell, or to cause any number of other mystical outcomes.

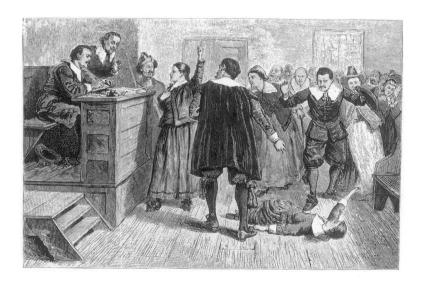

Above is a court in Salem, Massachusetts, where a hysterical young woman rolls on the floor as she accuses another woman of witchcraft. To the left is the title page of a pamphlet written by John Hale advising colonists of the dangers of witchcraft.

Witch hysteria did not originate in New England. It had begun in the Middle Ages and lasted into the eighteenth century in Europe. Native Americans and Africans had their own forms of "witchery." Many factors contributed to the disaster of the Salem witch trials. The desire to get even with one's neighbors may have been a factor. "Witches" (both men and women) became scapegoats. Some historians believe that the witch trials resulted from the feeling of panic that arose from the desire for individual freedoms and the waning of the Puritan influence. One of the more amazing aspects of the whole business is that those who claimed to be witches and "admitted" their guilt were usually spared while many of those who refused to admit to the charges were imprisoned or killed.

A Legacy

Most historians agree that the First Charter of Massachusetts and its subsequent history created a foundation for the democratic institutions that came after it. The Massachusetts Bay Company had led to the colony. Whether or not the charter gave the people of the colony the power to do so, they began to make their own laws.

The Massachusetts Bay colonists modified English laws according to their Puritan beliefs. To make their laws, the leaders of Massachusetts, along with the leaders of the other colonies, used precedents established in England. But they also put into practice certain ideas regarding government that were their own. The Massachusetts Bay Colony established some important principles of conduct and government.

Strange as it may seem, because of his strict belief system, John Calvin deserves much credit for leaving a legacy of democratic philosophy and institutions that continues in the New World. Calvin was one of those who believed that each person stands alone in the sight of God and that God, not a priest, gives salvation. This sense of individual responsibility is central to the American experiment.

Romantic notions persist about the Puritans and what they accomplished. The idea of freedom of thought and speech were strange and questionable to men of the Puritan era. However, many of our modern freedoms exist because of the Puritans' religious enthusiasm and their strong desire for self-government. In spite of the many challenges and mistakes of the leaders of the Massachusetts Bay Colony, and even after its failure as a religious state, the colony did succeed in establishing beliefs, traditions, and institutions of freedom that have endured to the present day.

The 1629 Charter of the Massachusetts Bay Colony

And further, That the said Governour and Companye, and their Successors, maie have forever one comon Seale, to be used in all Causes and Occasions of the said Company, and the same Seale may alter, chaunge, breake, and newe make, from tyme to tyme, at their pleasures. And our Will and Pleasure is, and Wee doe hereby for Us, our Heires and Successors, ordeyne and graunte, That from henceforth for ever, there shalbe one Governor, one Deputy Governor, and eighteene Assistants of the same Company, to be from tyme to tyme constituted, elected and chosen out of the Freemen of the saide Company, for the twyme being, in such Manner and Forme as hereafter in theis Presents is expressed, which said Officers shall applie themselves to take Care for the best disposeing and ordering of the generall buysines and Affaires of, for, and concerning the said Landes and Premisses hereby mentioned, to be graunted, and the Plantation thereof, and the Government of the People there. And for the better Execution of our Royall Pleasure and Graunte in this Behalf, Wee doe, by theis presents, for Us, our Heires and Successors, nominate, ordeyne, make, and constitute; our welbeloved the saide Mathewe Cradocke, to be the first and present

Governor of the said Company, and the saide Thomas Goffe, to be Deputy Governor of the saide Company, and the saide Sir Richard Saltonstall, Isaack Johnson, Samuell Aldersey, John Ven, John Humfrey, John Endecott, Simon Whetcombe, Increase Noell, Richard Pery, Nathaniell Wright, Samuell Vassall, Theophilus Eaton, Thomas Adams, Thomas Hutchins, John Browne, George Foxcrofte, William Vassall, and William Pinchion, to be the present Assistants of the saide Company, to continue in the saide several Offices respectivelie for such tyme, and in such manner, as in and by theis Presents is hereafter declared and appointed.

And further, Wee will, and by theis Presents, for Us, our Heires and Successors, doe ordeyne and graunte, That the Governor of the saide Company for the tyme being, or in his Absence by Occasion of Sicknes or otherwise, the Deputie Governor for the tyme being, shall have Authoritie from tyme to tyme upon all Occasions, to give order for the assembling of the saide Company, and calling them together to consult and advise of the Bussinesses and Affaires of the saide Company, and that the said Governor, Deputie Governor, and Assistants of the saide Company, for the tyme being, shall or maie once every Moneth, or oftener at their Pleasures, assemble and houlde and keepe a Courte or Assemblie of themselves, for the better ordering and directing of their Affaires, and that any seaven or more persons of the Assistants, togither with the Governor, or Deputie Governor soe assembled, shalbe saide, taken, held, and reputed to be, and shalbe a full and sufficient Courte or Assemblie of the said Company, for the handling, ordering, and dispatching of all such Buysinesses and Occurrents as shall from tyme to tyme happen, touching or concerning the. said Company or Plantation; and that there shall or maie be held and kept by the Governor, or Deputie Governor of the said Company, and seaven or more of the said Assistants for the tyme being, upon every last Wednesday in Hillary, Easter, Trinity, and Michas Termes respectivelie forever, one greate generall and solemne assemblie, which foure generall assemblies shalbe stiled and called the foure greate and generall Courts of the saide Company.

In all and every, or any of which saide greate and generall Courts soe assembled, Wee doe for Us, our Heires and Successors, give and graunte to the said Governor and Company, and their Successors, That the Governor, or in his absence, the Deputie Governor of the saide Company for the tyme being, and such of the Assistants and Freeman of the saide Company as shalbe present, or the greater nomber of them so assembled, whereof the Governor or Deputie Governor and six of the Assistants at the least to be seaven, shall have full Power and authoritie to choose, nominate, and appointe, such and soe many others as they shall thinke fitt, and that shall be willing to accept the same, to be free of the said Company and Body, and them into the same to admitt; and to elect and constitute such officers as they shall thinke fill and requisite, for the ordering, mannaging, and dispatching of the Affaires of the saide Governor and Company, and their Successors; And to make Lawes and Ordinances for the Good and Welfare of the saide Company, and for the Government and ordering of the saide Landes and Plantation, and the People inhabiting and to inhabite the same, as to them from tyme to tyme shalbe thought meete, soe as such Lawes and Ordinances be not contrarie or repugnant to the Lawes and Statuts of this our Realme of England.

And, our Will and Pleasure is, and Wee doe hereby for Us, our Heires and Successors, establish and ordeyne, That yearely once in the yeare, for ever hereafter, namely, the last Wednesday in Easter Tearme, yearely, the Governor, Deputy-Governor, and Assistants of the saide Company and all other officers of the saide Company shalbe in the Generall Court or Assembly to be held for that Day or Tyme, newly chosen for the Yeare ensueing by such greater parte of the said Company, for the Tyme being, then and there present, as is aforesaide. And, if it shall happen the present governor, Deputy Governor, and assistants, by theis presents appointed, or such as shall hereafter be newly chosen into their Roomes, or any of them, or any other of the officers to be appointed for the said Company, to dye, or to be removed from his or their severall Offices or Places before the saide generall Day of Election (whome Wee doe hereby declare for any Misdemeanor or Defect to be removeable by the Governor, Deputie Governor, Assistants, and Company, or such greater Parte of them in any of the publique Courts to be assembled as is aforesaid) That then, and in every such Case, it shall and maie be lawfull, to and for the Governor, Deputie Governor, Assistants, and Company aforesaide, or such greater Parte of them soe to be assembled as is aforesaide, in any of their Assemblies, to proceade to a new Election of one or more others of their Company in the Roome or Place, Roomes or Places of such Officer or Officers soe dyeing or removed according to their Discretions, And, immediately upon and after such Election and Elections made of such Governor, Deputie Governor, Assistant or Assistants, or any other officer of the saide Company, in Manner and Forme aforesaid, the Authoritie, Office, and Power, before given to the former Governor, Deputie Governor, or other Officer and Officers soe removed, in whose Steade and Place newe shalbe soe chosen, shall as to him and them, and everie of them, cease and determine

Provided alsoe, and our Will and Pleasure is, That aswell such as are by theis Presents appointed to be the present Governor, Deputie Governor, and Assistants of the said Company, as those that shall succeed them, and all other Officers to be appointed and chosen as aforesaid, shall, before they undertake the Execution of their saide Offices and Places respectivelie, take their Corporal Oathes for the due and faithfull Performance of their Duties in their severall Offices and Places, before such Person or Persons as are by theis Presents hereunder appointed to take and receive the same. . . .

And, further our Will and Pleasure is, and Wee doe hereby for Us, our Heires and Successors, ordeyne and declare, and graunte to the saide Governor and Company and their Successors, That all and every the Subjects of Us, our Heires or Successors, which shall goe to and inhabite within the saide Landes and hereby mentioned to be graunted, and every of their Children which shall happen to be borne there, or on the Seas in goeing thither, or retorning from thence, shall have and enjoy all liberties and Immunities of free and naturall Subjects within any of the Domynions of Us, our Heires or Successors, to all Intents, Constructions, and Purposes whatsoever, as if they and everie of them were borne within the Realme of England. And that the Governor and Deputie Governor of the said Company for the Tyme being, or either of them, and any two or more of such of the saide Assistants as shalbe thereunto appointed by the saide Governor and Company at any of their Courts or Assemblies to be held as aforesaide, shall

and maie at all Tymes, and from tyme to tyme hereafter, have full Power and Authoritie to minister and
give the Oathe and Oathes of Supremacie and Allegiance, or either of them, to all and everie Person and
Persons, which shall at any Tyme or Tymes hereafter
goe or passe to the Landes and Premisses hereby
mentioned to be graunted to inhabite in the same.

And, Wee doe of our further Grace, certen Knowledg
and meere Motion, give and graunte to the saide
Governor and Company, and their Successors, That it
shall and maie be lawfull, to and for the Governor or
Deputie Governor, and such of the Assistants and
Freemen of the said Company for the Tyme being as
shalbe assembled in any of their generall Courts aforesaide, or in any other Courtes to be specially sumoned
and assembled for that Purpose, or the greater Parte of
them (whereof the Governor or Deputie Governor, and
six of the Assistants to be alwaies seaven) from tyme to
tyme, to make, ordeine, and establishe all Manner of
wholesome and reasonable Orders, Lawes, Statutes,
and Ordinances, Directions, and Instructions, not
contrairie to the Lawes of this our Realme of England,
aswell for setling of the Formes and Ceremonies of
Government and Magistracy, fitt and necessary for the
said Plantation, and the Inhabitants there, and for name-
ing and setting of all sorts of Officers, both superior and
inferior, which they shall finde needefull for that
Governement and Plantation, and the distinguishing

and setting forth of the severall duties, Powers, and Lymytts of every such Office and Place, and the Formes of such Oathes warrantable by the Lawes and Statutes of this our Realme of England, as shalbe respectivelie ministred unto them for the Execution of the said severall Offices and Places; as also, for the disposing and ordering of the Elections of such of the said Officers as shalbe annuall, and of such others as shalbe to succeede in Case of Death or Removeall, and ministring the said Oathes to the newe elected Officers, and for Impositions of lawfull Fynes, Mulcts, Imprisonment, or other lawfull Correction, according to the Course of other Corporations in this our Realme of England, and for the directing, ruling, and disposeing of all other Matters and Thinges, whereby our said People, Inhabitants there, may be soe religiously, peaceablie, and civilly governed, as their good Life and orderlie Conversation, maie wynn and incite the Natives of Country, to the Knowledg and Obedience of the onlie true God and Savior of Mankinde, and the Christian Fayth, which in our Royall Intention, and the Adventurers free Profession, is the principall Ende of this Plantation.

Willing, commaunding, and requiring, and by theis Presents for Us, our Heires, and Successors, ordeyning and appointing, that all such Orders, Lawes, Statuts and Ordinances, Instructions and Directions, as shalbe soe made by the Governor, or Deputie Governor of the said Company, and such of the Assistants and Freemen as aforesaide, and published in Writing, under their common Seale, shalbe carefullie and dulie observed, kept, performed, and putt in Execution, according to the true Intent and Meaning of the same; and theis our Letters-patents, or the Duplicate or exemplification thereof, shalbe to all and everie such Officers, superior and inferior, from Tyme to Tyme, for the putting of the same Orders, Lawes, Statutes, and Ordinances, Instructions, and Directions, in due Execution against Us, our Heires and Successors, a sufficient Warrant and Discharge.

And Wee doe further, for Us, our Heires and Successors, give and graunt to the said Governor and Company, and their Successors by theis Presents, that all and everie such Chiefe Comaunders, Captaines, Governors, and other Officers and Ministers, as by the said Orders, Lawes, Statuts, Ordinances, Instructions, or Directions of the said Governor and Company for the Tyme being, shalbe from Tyme to Tyme hereafter imploied either in the Government of the saide Inhabitants and Plantation, or in the Waye by Sea thither, or from thence, according to the Natures and Lymitts of their Offices and Places respectively, shall from Tyme to Tyme hereafter for ever, within the Precincts and Partes of Newe England hereby mentioned to be graunted and confirmed, or in the Waie by Sea thither, or from thence, have full and

Absolute Power and Authoritie to correct, punishe, pardon, governe, and rule all such the Subjects of Us, our Heires and Successors, as shall from Tyme to Tyme adventure themselves in any Voyadge thither or from thence, or that shall at any Tyme hereafter, inhabite within the Precincts and Partes of Newe England aforasaid, according to the Orders, Lawes, Ordinances, Instructions, and Directions aforesaid, not being repugnant to the Lawes and Statutes of our Realme of England as aforesaid. . .

Glossary

antinomian One who believes that faith alone is necessary for salvation; anyone who rejects established religious authority.

authoritarian A political system in which people submit to a leader or group of leaders who hold most of the political power.

charter A written contract or agreement defining the rights and responsibilities between parties.

colony A group of people residing in a new territory that still maintains connections to the country from which the people have come.

commonwealth A nation or state united by agreement of the people, established for the common good of all.

enclosure The act of taking control of land and forcing the current occupants to leave.

nonconformist A person whose beliefs do not conform to those of the established church.

prophecy A prediction of some event to occur in the future, often based on reputed divine or religious powers.

Reformation A sixteenth-century religious
   movement that rejected the beliefs and rituals
   of the Roman Catholic Church.

shareholder A person who possesses certificates
   indicating ownership of a portion of a business.

For More Information

The Library of Congress
101 Independence Avenue SE
Washington, DC 20540
(202) 707-5000
Web site: http://www.loc.gov

Massachusetts Archives
220 Morrissey Boulevard
Boston, MA 02125
(617) 727-2816
Web site: http://www.state.ma.us/sec/arc/arcidx.htm

Massachusetts Historical Commission
220 Morrissey Boulevard
Boston, MA 02125
(617) 727-8470
Web site: http://www.state.ma.us/sec/mhc

The Massachusetts Historical Society
Secretary of the Commonwealth
1154 Boylston Street
Boston, MA 02215-3695
(617) 536-1608
Web site: http://www.masshist.org/index.html

National Archives and Records Administration
Northeast Regional Branch
Frederick C. Murphy Federal Center
380 Trapelo Road
Waltham, MA 02452-6399
(781) 647-8104
Web site: http://www.nara.gov/regional/boston.html

New England Historic Genealogical Society
101 Newbury Street
Boston, MA 02116-3007
(617) 536-5740
Web site: http://www.newenglandancestors.org

Smithsonian Institution
P. O. Box 37012
SI Building, Room 153
Washington, DC 20013-7012
(202) 357-2020
Web site: http://www.smithsonian.org

**The Society for the Preservation of
    New England Antiquities**
141 Cambridge Street
Boston, MA 02114
(617) 227-3956
Web site: http://www.spnea.org

The Winthrop Society
2690 Walker Avenue
Carmel, CA 93923
Web site: http://winthropsociety.org/home.htm

Web Sites

Due to the changing nature of Internet links, the
Rosen Publishing Group, Inc., has developed an
online list of Web sites related to the subject of this
book. This site is updated regularly. Please use this
link to access the list:

http://www.rosenlinks.com/gapd/cmbc

For Further Reading

Berkin, Carol. *First Generations: Women in Colonial America*. New York: Hill and Wang, 1996.

Collier, Christopher, and James L. Collier. *Pilgrims and Puritans*. New York: Benchmark Books, 1998.

Furbee, Mary R. *Outrageous Women of Colonial America*. New York: John Wiley & Sons, Inc., 2001.

Haskins, James, and Kathleen Benson. *Building a New Land: African Americans in Colonial America*. New York: HarperCollins Publishers, 2001.

Masoff, Joy. *Colonial Times 1600–1700*. New York: Scholastic, Inc., 2000.

Middleton, Richard. *Colonial America: A History, 1585–1776*, 2nd ed. Malden, MA: Blackwell Publishers, Inc., 1996.

Richter, Daniel K. *Facing East from Indian Country: A Native History of Early America*. Cambridge, MA: Harvard University Press, 2001.

Saari, Peggy. *Colonial America: Primary Sources*. Farmington Hills, MI: The Gale Group, 2000.

Sherman, Josepha. *The First Americans: Spirit of the Land and the People*. New York: Smithmark Publishers, 1996.

Stefoff, Rebecca. *The Colonies*. Tarrytown, NY: Marshall Cavendish Corporation, 2001.

Steins, Richard. *Colonial America*. New York: Raintree/ Steck-Vaughn Publishers, 2000.

Wood, Peter H. *Strange New Land: African-Americans 1617–1776*. New York: Oxford University Press, 1996.

Zinn, Howard. *A People's History of the United States, 1492–Present*. New York: HarperCollins, 1999.

Bibliography

Adams, Brooks. *The Emancipation of Massachusetts: The Dream and the Reality.* Boston: Houghton Mifflin Company, 1919.

Adams, James T. *Founding of New England.* Boston: The Atlantic Monthly Press, 1921.

Andrews, Charles M. *The Colonial Period of American History: The Settlements, Vol. 1.* New Haven, CT: Yale University Press, 1934.

Andrews, Charles M. *Our Earliest Colonial Settlements: Their Diversities of Origin and Later Characteristics.* Ithaca, NY: Cornell University Press, 1933.

Arber, Edward. *The Story of the Pilgrim Fathers, 1606–1633 A.D.; as told by Themselves, their Friends, and their Enemies.* Boston: Houghton Mifflin Company, 1897.

Breen, T. H. *Puritans and Adventurers: Change and Persistence in Early America.* New York: Oxford University Press, 1980.

Bremer, Francis J. *The Puritan Experiment: New England Society from Bradford to Edwards.* New York: St. Martin's Press, 1976.

Bridenbaugh, Carl. *Vexed and Troubled Englishmen 1590–1642: The Beginnings of the American People.* New York: Oxford University Press, 1968.

Emerson, Everett, ed. *Letters from New England: The Massachusetts Bay Colony, 1629–1638.* Amherst, MA: University of Massachusetts Press, 1987.

Fiske, John. *The Beginnings of New England, or, the Puritan Theocracy in its Relation to Civil and Religious Liberty.* Boston: Houghton Mifflin Company, 1917.

French, Allen. *Charles I and the Puritan Upheaval.* Boston: Houghton Mifflin Company, 1955.

Haskins, George L. *Law and Authority in Early Massachusetts: A Study in Tradition and Design.* New York: Archon Books, 1968.

Koehler, Lyle. *A Search for Power: The "Weaker Sex" in Seventeenth-Century New England.* Champaign, IL: University of Illinois Press, 1980.

Middleton, Richard. *Colonial America: A History, 1585–1776*, 2nd ed. Malden, MA: Blackwell Publishers, Inc., 1996.

Mitchell, Stewart, ed. *The Founding of Massachusetts: A Selection from the Sources of the History of the Settlement 1628–1631.* Boston: The Massachusetts Historical Society, 1930.

Morgan, Edmund S., ed. *The Founding of Massachusetts: History and the Sources.* Indianapolis, IN: The Bobbs-Merrill Company, Inc., 1964.

Palfrey, John G. *Compendious History of New England from the Discovery by Europeans to the First General Congress of the Anglo-American colonies, Vol. 1.* Boston: Houghton Mifflin Company, 1873.

Pomfret, John E., and Floyd M Shumway. *Founding the American Colonies: 1583–1660.* New York: Harper & Row Publishers, 1970.

Vaughan, Alden T., ed. *The Puritan Tradition in America: Documentary History of the United States.* Columbia, SC: University of South Carolina Press, 1972.

Winthrop, John. *Winthrop Papers 1498–1628, Vol. I.* Boston: Massachusetts Historical Society, 1929.

Ziff, Larzer. *Puritanism in America: New Culture in a New World.* New York: American Heritage Publishing Co., Inc., 1961.

Ziner, Feenie. *The Pilgrims and Plymouth Colony.* New York: American Heritage Publishing Co., Inc., 1961.

Primary Source
Image List

Page 9: A colored woodblock print of Martin Luther by Lucas Cranach the Elder, created sometime in the 1540s, now housed at the Germanisches Nationalmuseum, Nuremberg, Germany.

Page 10: A lithograph printed in 1874 by H. Breul, based on a painting of H. Bruckner, showing the life of Martin Luther and other heroes of the Reformation. A copy is housed in the Library of Congress.

Page 14: The title page of *The Book of Common Prayer*, the 1662 edition by Thomas Cranmer. A copy is in the Library of Congress.

Page 22: An advertisement from the English pamphlet *Nova Britannia*, printed in 1609.

Page 26: A colored print of John Smith (c. 1580 to 1631).

Page 27: A print showing settlers arriving at Jamestown, made in 1807.

Page 29: A nineteenth-century painting by Jean Leon Gerome Ferris depicting the signing of the Mayflower Compact in 1620.

Page 30: The Mayflower Compact, signed in 1620.

Page 33: A painting of Charles I receiving benediction before his execution. Below is the order of execution dated January 29, 1649. It is now housed in the Houses of Parliament in London.

Page 36: An engraving of John Endicott, acting governor of the Massachusetts Bay Colony until 1630.

Page 38: A painting of Governor William Bradford interrupting the revelers at Merrymount.

Page 40: The Charter of the Massachusetts Bay Colony, adopted in 1629.

Page 43: A portrait of John Winthrop by Amos Doolittle (1754-1832). It is housed at the National Portrait Gallery of the Smithsonian Institution in Washington, DC.

Page 44: The opening page of John Winthrop's *Considerations for the Plantation of New England*, published in 1622, now housed in the Library of Congress.

Page 49: A painting of John Winthrop aboard the *Arbella*.

Page 51: The remains of the *Sparrow-Hawk*, wrecked in 1626. The hull is now on exhibit in Pilgrim Hall, in Plymouth, Massachusetts.

Page 53: A painting of the Pilgrims arriving at Plymouth Harbor in 1620.

Page 63: *The Bloody Tenent of Persecution*, by Roger Williams, published in 1644. A copy can be found at the Library of Congress.

Page 64: A print showing the trial of Anne Hutchinson in 1637.

Page 67: A print showing the burning of a Pequot village in 1637.

Page 68: A view of Harvard College in 1668, drawn in 1935.

Page 70: *The General Laws and Liberties of the Massachusets Colony*, printed in 1672. A copy is in the Library of Congress.

Page 75: *The Indian Bible of John Eliot*, published in 1663. A copy is housed in the Harvard College Library.

Page 83: The title page from *A Modest Enquiry into the Nature of Witchcraft, and how persons guilty of that crime may be convicted: and the means used for their discovery discussed, both negatively and affirmatively, according to Scripture and experience.* by John Hale, published in 1702.

Index

About the Author

Barbara Moe is the author of numerous books for young adults. She is a long-time history buff who currently lives in Colorado with her husband and their two dogs, Missy and Angel.

Credits

Editor

Jake Goldberg

Design and Layout

Les Kanturek